Poetry in Motion

Leicester

Edited by Donna Samworth

CW01018786

 Young**Writers**

First published in Great Britain in 2004 by:
Young Writers
Remus House
Coltsfoot Drive
Peterborough
PE2 9JX
Telephone: 01733 890066
Website: www.youngwriters.co.uk

All Rights Reserved

© Copyright Contributors 2004

SB ISBN 1 84460 378 4

Foreword

This year, the Young Writers' 'Poetry In Motion' competition proudly presents a showcase of the best poetic talent selected from over 40,000 up-and-coming writers nationwide.

Young Writers was established in 1991 to promote the reading and writing of poetry within schools and to the youth of today. Our books nurture and inspire confidence in the ability of young writers and provide a snapshot of poems written in schools and at home by budding poets of the future.

The thought effort, imagination and hard work put into each poem impressed us all and the task of selecting poems was a difficult but nevertheless enjoyable experience.

We hope you are as pleased as we are with the final selection and that you and your family continue to be entertained with *Poetry In Motion Leicester* for many years to come.

Contents

Sir Jonathan North Community College

Stonehill High School

William Bradford Community College

The Poems

Pass On A Smile

As I walked the dog today,
With a smile upon my face,
I noticed that I'd passed it on,
Like relays in a race.

Then as I walked further on,
With a grin from ear to ear,
I thought how nice it was to see a smile,
And it fills you with good cheer.

A smile doesn't cost a thing,
And it isn't hard to do,
Just try it on some passers-by,
And you'll get them smiling too.

The world would be a nicer place,
And troubles would seem small,
If smiling became an epidemic,
And was proudly worn by all.

Rose Balment (11)
Brookvale High School

Why?

Why do birds sing in trees?
Why do we pray on our knees?
Why do people love and hate, in this life?

Why does time never stand still?
Why do murderers want to kill?
Why does everything have to die, in this life?

Why does peace never commence?
Why does the world make no sense?
Why do people love and hate, in this life?

Sophie Graham (13)
Brookvale High School

Alone Again

They stood,
Cursing every step of my approach,
Their scowls,
Like girders upon their brows,
Their icy tongues,
Whipped at my soul,
Like pillars they stood,
Colossal against my cowering stature,
Like a ghost I fled,
I fled through the fields,
I fled through the streets,
There I stood,
Alone again!

Andrew Stones (14)
Brookvale High School

World War II

World War II, on the battlefields men tried,
On the battlefields men died.
The fight was over land
And then grew into World War II.

1939, declared was war,
1945, war was no more.
People mourned the souls that they knew,
From that evil phase, World War II.

We still remember the people that fought bravely,
November the 11th is the day.
We also remember the planes that dropped bombs,
Then flew, from that part of life,
                              World War II.

Sophie Brewster (11)
Brookvale High School

Cradle Song

A newborn child lies sleeping silently,
Not knowing what life may spring,
A newborn child, so gentle and unaware
Of the troubles this world may bring.

I warn the child to have a gleeful life,
With a spirit of great and happy cause,
I warn the child to be honest and truthful
And to never break any laws.

I advise the child to face up to what it believes in,
To have a mind of its own,
I advise the child to take life as it is
And try not to whine or groan.

I preach to the child to accept others,
Even if they are spiteful and unkind,
I preach to the child to not be ignorant
And to have a thoughtful mind.

I tell the child of what dangers may come,
To avoid any risk of death,
I tell the child to live life as full as possible
But to save its own breath.

A newborn child lies sleeping silently,
Now knowing what life may spring,
A newborn child so gentle but aware
Of the troubles this world may bring.

Lucy Whitehead (13)
Brookvale High School

The Day The Emotions Went To War

It started of course with anger
It marched thunderously on the unoffending
Cutting them down with hate and wrath
Its nightmare army of harsh words descending.

Then came doleful sadness
Flooding the plain of fury
It leeched its way through every strand of resentment
It brought wistfulness, they were sorry.

The battle was almost over,
But pride came marching in,
It silenced the words of penitence, built high defensive tales
Left war to begin again.

Sadness' mournful army lay in siege
But pride's high walls stood unshaken
Time stood still in stalemate but then,
Guilt came with its grappling hooks.

Pride's defences didn't stand a chance
They crumbled unwillingly
And forgiveness and pardon came pouring out
Friendship and peace came joyously.

Rachael Scott (12)
Brookvale High School

The Scarecrow

There's a scarecrow across the road
That gives all the birds a fright.
Just standing in the same place,
All day and all night.
I always see that scarecrow,
Standing out, so yellow,
In thunder, rain and sun,
From my window.
That poor scarecrow, it cannot move,
Not able to go walking or dance in a groove.
I feel sorry for that lonely scarecrow,
Out there protecting the seeds.
If I could give him anything,
A friend is what he needs.

James Wright (11)
De Lisle Catholic Science College

Light Bulb

Old tapes
Reminiscent
Of who I was,
Nostalgic melody

Fading.

Dead moth,
A dry corpse
It clutches a
Velvet curtain.
Stiff like tree bark

What if

It falls?
It will fall
And when it does,
It will fall to pieces.

So will I
One day . . .
One day soon

Crushed wings
Snapped legs
Broken

I will be
I will fly again
I will find myself.

Hugh Escott (17)
De Lisle Catholic Science College

My Friend

S kye is nice
K ind and sweet
Y es, she is my girlfriend
E ager to please

M arvellous at hide-and-seek
A lways fun to be with
N ever nasty
S hares her toys
H elpful
I s good at home
P erfect.

Ben Ogden (12)
Ellesmere College

William

W illiam is kind,
I s helpful,
L ikes to play Ludo.
L earns to ride his bike,
I s good to people,
A lways a good friend,
M arvellous at playing games.

Daniel Harrison (12)
Ellesmere College

Summer 2003

This summer it was really hot
And guess what?
Every day I played out
My friends would all shout!

Kerry Litchfield (12)
Ellesmere College

Karl

K ind to his friends
A lways listens
R uns well in games
L ikes sweets.

Tiash Patel (12)
Ellesmere College

Kind Karl

K ind Karl
A friendly person
R eally quiet
L ikes to laugh.

S ensible
T rustworthy
O bedient
N ice to his friends
E veryone's favourite
S uper to know.

Mark Cross (13)
Ellesmere College

Summer 2003

This summer in Spain
There was no rain
We went to the pub at night
Where the lights were bright.

Laura Khan (13)
Ellesmere College

Summer 2003

This summer I went to France on a boat.
When I got to Paris I wrote a note,
To tell my friend I'd floated on a boat.

Khalil Sheikh (12)
Ellesmere College

Mark

M ark makes me laugh
A lways smiling
R uns fast
K ind to me.

Karl Stones (13)
Ellesmere College

Robot Spy

It was a cold, dark night
When I came down from space
I'm made out of metal
Scientists control me from planet Pluto
My mission is to spy on human beings
Taking it back to space . . .

Vijay Naik
Ellesmere College

Snowball

All the animals love me,
They see me as their leader,
They honour and respect me,
They have to, I'm their reader.

My dreams are just as follows,
I'll be leaving them soon you'll see,
I will fill all that is hollow,
And declare all animals free.

I will lead us to equality,
I will live Old Major's dream,
I will complete my noble duty
All animals together in a team.

Follow me, my comrades,
I will break all man-made chains,
That restrain us from our freedom,
Man the barricades!

Ayesha Sharda (13)
Judgemeadow Community College

Untitled

The ground is frosted beneath my feet
Silence lingering in the sky
In contrast to the funky beat
Blaring from the house nearby

A celebration, a party, to support a new year
People cheering, a countdown with increasing fear
What is to come, what will time bring?
No one cares, just cart champagne in

We all say, 'Let the good times roll'
An excuse to get hammered, not feel the cold
An exhilarating atmosphere, intense mood
Forget to sulk, get angry, brood

Echoing music raising the degrees
Masking the darkness, the cold breeze.

Helena Dowson (15)
Judgemeadow Community College

The End

The world can end
It can end today
It can even end tomorrow

It will end in blood
It will end in fire
It will even end in anguish

The day shall be dark
And full of death
And people being possessed

Satan shall come
To claim his prey
While, the world is ending in anguish.

A horse will ride across the sky
And people will stare with hope
But all this means is the end has come
The end has come today.

Sunil Mistry (15)
Judgemeadow Community College

Britain!

There was a country called Britain
Which was set up in the United Kingdom.
First it was small,
And then it was big,
Now there are over 50 million.
Lots of people live there,
But I don't know where
Because there are lots of people!

Kareema Modan (12)
Judgemeadow Community College

The Sad Truth

Ah, Christmas Day,
No time for work, just play.
Children running, snowballs flying,
'Merry Christmas,' people say.

But underneath the joy,
A man's best friend just died.
He could have had a great life,
Instead he had to cry.

Dogs, cats, rabbits, sheep,
Hamsters, birds and mice,
They may be very cute things,
Why aren't they treated nice?

From testing to abandoning,
Nobody seems to care.
Some madmen even think
The whole thing's pretty fair.

So next time you see a dog,
Don't drown it down in litmus,
Because a dog is for life
Not just for Christmas.

Rikesh Mistry (13)
Judgemeadow Community College

Ken The Kangaroo And Starfish

Ken the Kangaroo

Ken the kangaroo came from Sydney
And what a great jumper he was too,
We thought he was amazing,
And that was true,
He could jump over fences,
As if they weren't there.
When they picked the animal athletics
He was top of the list.

Starfish

Spined with sparks,
Limbed with flames,
Climbing the dark to cling and shine,
Until the slow tide turns away,
Not even knowing what stars are,
But even so, the same.

Inderjit Nagra (12)
Judgemeadow Community College

The Tiger

A tiger who's burning bright,
In the forests of the night,
A tiger with big, black stripes,
A tiger who's brave like a knight.

A tiger who's got a coat bright fired,
The coat that might attract others,
Its eyes are brightly fierce,
Which will make others fearfully scared.

Nisha Tailor (12)
Judgemeadow Community College

Animals

Some animals suffer every day,
In every possible, deadly way.
Being tested on for drugs,
And then catching nasty bugs.
Some are locked up in cages,
For ages and ages.
All animals want is some loyalty,
But instead they lose their family.

Bhupinder Kaur Mann (12)
Judgemeadow Community College

Afraid

Here I am stuck
Inside of this cage,
I hope they don't hurt me,
I am so afraid.
Men in white suits keep walking by,
Whispering an evil whisper.
They walk back again with a new animal,
'Where are they going?'
I hope no one will hurt me,
I am so afraid.

Thomasina Jordan-Rhodes (13)
Judgemeadow Community College

Home Is The Place

I was born here,
Here is my home.
Home is my place.
Place I know and love.
Love is the best word.
Word, the place is Britain
Britain is my home
Home, I know and love.

Amy Jones (13)
Judgemeadow Community College

Vivisection

Vivisection is very bad,
The people that do it are very mad,
The animals get really sad,
For all the good times they could have had.
The cats and dogs are very sad,
Because they're locked in their cages,
They've tried to get out for several years,
But they've been there for ages.

Zeyn Tayub (12)
Judgemeadow Community College

Etched in My Mind

The crisp autumn day
As normal as any other
Etched in my mind

The plane hurtling towards us
The worried and confused murmurs
Etched in my mind

The explosion as the plane hit
The horror that flowed over me
Etched in my mind

The hysterical screams
The stampede of terrified workers
Etched in my mind

The cries of trapped colleagues
My conscience urging me to stay
Etched in my mind.

Fayola Francis (13)
Sir Jonathan North Community College

How Can That Be?

How can it be
That they do the same work
But he gets paid more?

How can it be
That they go on the same date
But he gets to pay?

How can it be
That they live in the same house
But she does all the chores?

How can it be
That she is more efficient than him
But he gets promoted first?

How can that be?

Verity Moody (13)
Sir Jonathan North Community College

I Worry

I worry that you will leave me
I worry that you will no longer love me
I worry that you don't understand
I worry that I can't understand
I worry that you are too perfect
So perfect that this is a dream
I worry that I love you more than you love me
Then you come to see me
I don't worry.

Maya Lamoudi (13)
Sir Jonathan North Community College

Hunted

'Witch,' they scream, they shout, they yell.
I was a rock, too late, I fell.
They've got me now, I know my fate.
He comes towards me, I look up and wait.
I can see it already, the deadly flame
'Devil's child,' he spits, like it's my name.
He kicks my shin, he grabs my arm.
If I really were a witch, I'd do him harm.
'It's Hell for you!' he spits, his breath on my face.
It's up I know it. The end of the chase.
I'm thrown into a cell. It's damp, smelly, dark.
I dread the fire, I sense the spark.
I feel the lick and beat off the fire.
I plead my case but they call me a liar.
He comes for me, pulls me out by the hair,
Out of the stench in my cell, I gasp for air.
'Enjoy it,' he growls, 'it'll be your last!
You'll burn from now till forever,' he drags me out fast.
A crowd has gathered around the stage where I'll die,
I'm scared, I whimper, but I swear I won't cry.
They tie me to a pole, the crowd is calling.
I shut my eyes, I feel like I'm falling.
Deep into a dark and empty pit,
My life is ending, this is it!
I'm all tied up now, they're lighting the wood,
Some people are leaving, I wish that I could.
I can barely breathe for all the smoke,
The witch-hunter laughs like it's one big joke.
The fire's high now, so hot, my eyes stream,
I open my mouth and just scre- . . . *I'm gone!*

Catherine Watson (13)
Sir Jonathan North Community College

When I Lost You

When I lost you,
It was like a feather falling from the sky,
Floating down from way up high.

When I lost you,
It was like a trodden-on rose,
Lost the love of my life, the one that I chose.

When I lost you,
It was like losing the head of the pride,
I needed you to be my guide.

Years ago I lost you,
Now the photos will always remind,
Of the love from you that again I won't find.

Eve Harding (13)
Sir Jonathan North Community College

A Loving Story At Christmas!

The whipper winds whipped
upon their frost morn.
It's Christmas!
The presents all neat in rows.
The food prepared, so-so.
It's Christmas!
The decorations stand high
in the moonlit sky.
It's Christmas!
One little girl in an orphanage
stands alone by the fridge
waiting for someone to love her.
Finally someone comes to be her
best-ever chum.
Everyone shouts,
'It's Christmas!'

Abigail Platts (13)
Sir Jonathan North Community College

Dream

Bright candlelight,
Opens the mist,
Where I see a cottage,
Which I've not seen before.
I walk up close,
And slowly open the door,
To see nothing,
But a dark brown floor.
I walk in aware,
Of nothing but me,
But a loud noise scares me,
I flee,
I run, I run,
I go so fast,
Then I wake up,
Oh, at last!

Laura Tilley (14)
Sir Jonathan North Community College

Let Me Be . . .

Let me be your joke book,
To make you laugh and smile.
Let me be your telephone,
I'll listen when you dial.
Let me be your candle,
There to light your way.
Let me be your broomstick,
To brush your fears away.
Let me be your trophy,
Standing tall and proud.
Let me be your limo,
Carrying you around.
Let me be your chocolate bar,
Comforting and sweet.
Let me be your loving heart,
Never skip a beat.
Let me be your medicine,
When you are in pain.
Let me be your umbrella,
Protecting you in rain.

Naomi Willett (13)
Sir Jonathan North Community College

You Were There

When I was all alone,
No one there,
The darkness surrounding me,
No one to care,
You were there,
Shining your light,
Through the darkness,
Making it ever so bright.

Oh, when I was busy,
With clubs and friends, still,
You stayed by my side,
And loved me as you always will.

Alice Gray (13)
Sir Jonathan North Community College

Sheep

The grass looks inviting and delicate
But is sharp as a dagger
This shows that these sheep
Are no softies.
The sheep go *chomp, chomp* on the grass.
Fluffy and white as a cloud are they,
Sweet-looking like chocolate.
The sheep go *chomp, chomp* on the grass.
'Thick as a plank,' some would say,
But they don't know
To what extent these sheep will go,
To get what they want.
The sheep go *chomp, chomp* on the grass.
Frolicking in spring and across fields the lambs do go.
'Oh how cute,' some people would say,
Then to go and eat a whole plate of chops!
The sheep go *chomp, chomp* on the grass.
Playing 'follow the leader', bleating the enemy,
Running rings around the sheepdog.
Are these sheep really stupid?
The sheep go *chomp, chomp* on the grass.
There's an open gate and a dozy farmer,
Across hill and dale they go,
Through the meadows and over the brook
Because
Grass awaits
On the other side.
So are these sheep really so stupid?
The sheep go *chomp, chomp* on the grass.
The sheep go *chomp, chomp* on the grass.

Emma Sainthouse (13)
Sir Jonathan North Community College

Watching From The Sidelines

(Written from personal experience)

And another brilliant steal from GD
GD passes to C who passes to WA who passes to . . .
Not me, never me because I'm benched.

A fantastic shot from GA
A magnificent intercept from GD
No chance to dive, no chance to shoot
Because I'm benched.

No shouts from a treacherous teacher
No cheers for an excellent defence
No time to get sweaty, no time to get ready
Because I'm benched.

And GK manages to steal the ball
A shot she prevents.
And whilst others around me are picked
I'm permanently benched.

To please understand Ms Lowther that I'm not ecstatic
- Act like this win was a godsend,
Because throughout the passing, scoring, intercepting,
Fouling, cheering, rebounding and marking,
I was benched!

Liberty Heskeymee-Preston (14)
Sir Jonathan North Community College

Leopard

Leopard stalks, crawls, glides,
Dashes across the open plain;
Terror, momentum and thrill of the chase,
The beating of bongos gives rhythm to the game.
A game so deadly, yet so well planned,
A foot for a foot, an eye for an eye, a tooth for a tooth,
And a life for a life.
Yearning to tear, to rip, to kill,
Yearning for never-ending triumph,
One pounce, one strike, one bite,
The game is over.
Blood seeps across the mud.
Wind blows bare, the red flesh,
Hunger dies for one night at least,
Until the whole fearsome game starts over again.
Come morning, a bird awakens,
Oblivious to the night before.

Alexander Garton (12)
Stonehill High School

Jaguar

Perfect stillness,
A hot blanket smothers the rainforest,
A shiver in the bushes,
Toucans crow from high treetops,
A shuddering breath is drawn.

Suddenly, a sleek black bullet,
Streaks across the clearing,
In a flash of white teeth and gleaming eyes,
Like a bolt of electricity,
The antelope jump and turn.

The trees form a deadly barrier,
Enclosing the antelope with their death,
In a mad frenzy they crash about in terror,
Blood splatters the dry ground.

Rosa Theobald (12)
Stonehill High School

The Way Of The Water

The swirling, whirling world of whirlpools,
Spinning down the plughole.
A frothing mass of water,
Waiting to hit the drain.

The gurgle of the water,
As it rushes through the pipes,
Dragging dirt along with it,
As it rushes to the end.

The water crashes to a halt,
Leaking through gaps in the wire mesh.
Then the whirlpool starts again,
Gushing its way to the sewer.

Nicola Smart (12)
Stonehill High School

German Shepherds

When they sit down
They have got a big frown.
When it's time for a walk
They start to talk.
Their fur is shiny and long
It proves they're healthy and strong.
Their nose is long and wide.
They hold their head with pride.
They have eyes that shine.
They twinkle in the night.
Their eyes are all starry,
They glare in the light.
They make you quiver.
Their teeth are big and sharp
And make you shiver.
Their paws are like stones
When they are fully grown.

Mary-Jane Crowfoot (14)
William Bradford Community College

How Long Will They Mourn Me?

If you have a special friend, love him with all your heart.
You'll never know when the day will come,
When you will have to part.
Memories that will be treasured.
Your smile so unique.
From the day they took you, they knew you needed sleep.
Hearts will always be broken,
Tears will always weep.
But what I would give for you, just to wake you from your sleep.

Ashley Willden (14)
William Bradford Community College

My Teenage Life

My life is spinning out of my hands,
I am not sure where it will land.
One day I could be really sad,
Other days I will be extremely bad.

I often stress out,
But I don't know what about.
I take it out on my mum,
Normally it starts out as a bit of fun.

My mood's likely to change,
And I find it very strange.
One minute I will be as high as a kite,
The next I could be in a fight.

I wish I could change the way I am,
I often feel like a timid lamb.
I used to be happy and normal,
But since thirteen I've felt abnormal.

My mum blames it on my teenage years,
These have caused a lot of fears.
Often she says it's because I'm a girl,
But my moods are like a great big twirl!

Fiona Paxton (15)
William Bradford Community College

What Life's About!

It won't be long till I get old,
Sitting there, wrinkly and bald,
So I'm going to enjoy life,
Make sure there's no strife,
Make every moment count,
Isn't that what life's about?

Natasha Overton (14)
William Bradford Community College

Penalty

The final minutes are here
The referee's whistle blows in my ear
'Penalty!' he says, pointing to the spot
Our hopes of winning begin to rot

The striker on the opposite team, bravely steps up
If he misses, we win the Cup
He hits the ball without any fear
It sails over the bar, we begin to cheer!

Ashley Morris (14)
William Bradford Community College

A Wish

If I had a wish
    A wish that would come true
        A wish that no one else knew
            I'd wish for you
            But if you had a wish
        A wish that would come true
    A wish no one else knew
Would it be the same for you?
    And if, it would,
        How would I know it was you
            Who felt the same way about me
        As I do for you?

Terri Musson (14)
William Bradford Community College

Now

At first my heart was full
Then you once told me, 'No.'
From then my life was dull
I can't believe you!

I wanted you to be near
My desires burned bright
Other girls I fear
I can't believe you!

My friend, you hurt me bad,
You split my heart in two
No more tears were to be had
I can't believe you!

Why did you have to go
And make me this way
Although I feel low
I
    Am
         Stronger!

Lauren Preston (14)
William Bradford Community College

My Mum

When I'm ill she cares for me
When I'm sad she's there for me
Whenever she's not around
I feel like sinking into the ground
She loves me, that's all I need to know
When I'm feeling sad and low
So this poem that I hum
Is definitely about my mum.

Laura Kelly (14)
William Bradford Community College

Music

Standing in the crowd
I wait, I wait
For the band to start
I wait, I wait
The band comes out.
The crowd goes wild.

They play their guitars
The floor vibrates
The drums come in
They start to sing

The crowd gets closer
I start to get hot
It is so loud my ears start to pop
The solo gets closer
I wait, I wait
For the crowd to go wild
I wait, I wait
He plays the solo
It sounds great

They finish the song
They leave us with a cheer
It starts getting cold
As the people leave.

Casey Simpson (14)
William Bradford Community College

The Prey

As it waited, watching its food,
Walking around near the lakeside,
Slowly getting closer and closer,
Ready to make the kill.

As it watched, one of the deer
Moved away from the rest of the group.
It knew that now was the time to eat.
It approached the deer from behind,
It got ready to jump.
Just at the last second it heard a bang!
It was the hunters.
It ran away, to attack the deer another day.

Michael Keddy (14)
William Bradford Community College

Haunted

At night I was in bed asleep
I was having a nightmare in deep sleep
I woke up hearing noises
And heard many strange voices
I stood up suddenly and went to see
I went closer and closer, what was it meant to be?
I saw him there standing still, looking very mean.
He was standing against the wall looking very lean.
He raised one hand, ready to strike
And demanded my name, I replied it was Mike
I ran from home
Until I was safe and alone
And since that day I've been haunted.

Niket Mistry (14)
William Bradford Community College

Nikki

Her eyes, twinkling in the morning light
Her voice, a swift note in a song
Her body, an elegant landscape of pure art
Her lips, rose texture, I dare not touch
Her hair, windswept within the cool breeze
I stare at her across the classroom
Wishing she was mine
But never in a million years
Will I get a girl so fine.

Jack Watson (14)
William Bradford Community College

Olympic Gold Medal

Do you know about wrestling?
Probably not
Do you want to know about wrestling?
Well I know a lot
I know the heights of the tallest
The year they were born
The size of the smallest
And what muscles they've torn
I can tell you their names
How much they weigh
All of their actions
And everything they say
The accidents and injuries
Each one has sustained
All the belts and medals
Each one has gained
I want to wrestle
One day that'll be me
The Olympics first
I'll be the best of the three
With my medal of gold
Raised to the sky
Listening to the cheer
With my head held high
I knew I would make it
Well, I'm finally there.

Luke Hanks (14)
William Bradford Community College

Dear Racist

Dear Racist,

I'm black, OK, so what's your problem?
We're made of the same things,
A heart, two eyes and skin.

I've lived here all my life,
But so have you.
What gives you the right to say it's your country?
That I don't belong? It hurts.

You should try living in war and poverty,
Scared for the next day.
What will happen?
I prepare to grieve.

It hurts when you call me
Names with no thought,
You think of a black man
And suddenly . . . you change,
Something comes over you,
You call me names, spit and yell.
It hurts me to hear you knock me.

But what gives you the right?
You don't know me at all,
I'm just like you,
I'm different, that's all.

Do you knock your friends
Because their hair's not like yours?
Do you mock your family,
When they're not the same?

You're not all naïve,
Most are kind and good,
Respect for my skin, my blood.

But those simple few
Who can't see through,
Make me feel unwanted,
Even though I know it's not true.

To be honest, you're shallow,
Not seeing beneath my skin,
I'm just like you,
A heart, two eyes and skin.

Brioney Worthington (14)
William Bradford Community College

Running

Sometimes I ask myself why it is so important to me.
Maybe it's the thrill, the excitement, the uncertainty.
Maybe the hard work which I put into it.
Maybe it's the achievement, the rewards I aim for.
Maybe I do it for the challenge.
Maybe it's the bitter pill of failure.
Maybe it's the acceleration of the chase.
Maybe it tells me what sort of person I am.
Maybe.

Edward James Highton (14)
William Bradford Community College

Being A Fish

I swim round and round my bowl all day,
Wondering what I would say,
If I was a human and I could talk,
And where I would go if I could walk,
It's like being in a prison cell,
But don't get me wrong, they treat me well,
They feed and talk to me every day,
But why, oh why, did they take me away
From my friends and family in the sea?
Oh, how happy they must be,
To be swimming freely all day long,
Swimming around where they belong,
How I miss making bubbles and having fun,
With my friends under the sun,
Beaming through the cool, calm sea,
But I am here lonely as can be,
And now I know what I would say,
And it would be 'Have a nice day,
And think about how you would feel
If you were a fish taken away and concealed,
Inside a bowl forever more,
And kept as a pet and be always bored,
And you know, you are going to die,
Without even saying goodbye
To your friends, so what do you do?
Pretend you're dead and be flushed down the loo,
So then now hopefully,
You will end up where you should be,
In the sea where you belong,
To swim freely all day long.'

Emily Walker (14)
William Bradford Community College

Shopping Spree

It's Saturday today
Yesterday I got my pay,
My mates are all coming round
With money, lots of pounds.
We'll catch the bus at eleven
Be there for shopping heaven.

We shop around for hours
For clothes we wish were ours,
Trousers and tops,
Boots and flip-flops,
We could be here for hours!

At one, we break for lunch,
Sandwiches, chips, what shall we munch?
We don't take long to eat
'Cause we can't wait to get back on our feet.

The shops are calling us back
We avoid the shops that are tack.
I buy a dress of crimson-red,
Flowing with elegance from toe to head.

The shops have all become bare,
But we are still standing there.
As the clock turns to five,
The shops are no longer alive.

We dash to catch the bus,
Our shopping trips are a must,
Next week we'll come back for more,
Shop till we drop on the floor!

Emily Roper (14)
William Bradford Community College

Invisible

Lost and alone,
In a world so dull and cold,
She has nothing to her name,
And nobody to hold.

She curls up in the rain,
On a torn blanket on the floor,
Nobody seems to care about her,
She's just something they ignore.

An outcast, a loner, a tramp,
Carelessly cast aside,
She is caught in a trap by poverty,
Nowhere to run or hide.

She longs for a way out,
That she could just fade away,
A bottle of pills could end it all,
Nobody would miss her anyway!

Kelly Brown (14)
William Bradford Community College

Why?

Why is there war in the world? *Why* can't there be peace?
Why is there illness that we can't cure?
Why do we die? *Why* can't we live forever?
Why is there racism?
Why is there starvation?
Why do we not respect our surroundings?
Why do we have rich and poor?
Why do we have good and bad?
Why do we feel love? *Why* do we feel hate?
Why do we laugh? *Why* do we cry?
Why is there bullying? *Why* can't we all just get along?
Why can't everyone be treated equally?

Why don't people believe in the person who knows all the answers?

Danielle Holder (14)
William Bradford Community College

Football

Football is great, the vibe when you score
the cheers from the fans are like roaring lions
the boos from the opposition sound like a herd of cows mooing
the bone-crunching tackles flying in like planes landing at an airport
the cards being shown by the ref like a poker game
the whistle blowing at full-time
the winning team cheering with the fans.

Ross Wilson (14)
William Bradford Community College

The Apocalypse!

A morphous alien beings capturing children and never letting them free.

P ain spreading mercilessly throughout the world.

O phidian creatures injecting their deadly venom into every living thing in their paths.

C olossal amounts of panic and fear possess the human race.

A nkle-deep in blood, men are driven insane.

L ittle demons tricking people into terrifying traps.

Y eti-type animals rip bodies apart.

P eople are united and attempt to resist but they are crushed instantly.

S ounds of screams and wails fill the land.

E verything alive has been destroyed and the planet is doomed!

Gareth Roy (14)
William Bradford Community College

A Dream To Remember

I have a talent
To live or let die
The power I have
But I don't know why
The dream I won't forget.

For generations it has
Been passed down
The power is within me
To save this town
The dream I won't forget.

I have a brother
Who will help me
We have to fight it
Written in this prophecy
The dream I won't forget.

Soon the end of life
Will be here
I will conquer
Without fear
The dream I won't forget.

This power of mine
Is the best
I can fly higher
Than the rest
The dream I won't forget.

Sean Webb-Harris
William Bradford Community College

Life's Not Scary

Shadows everywhere
Noises down the street
It doesn't scare me.
Everyone shouting
But I'm OK.

Ghosts come in nightmares
And in another way or form.
It doesn't scare me,
Even when they make me jump
But I'm OK.

Drunken animals staggering
From the pub,
Walking down dark alleys
All alone.
It doesn't scare me.

Creatures small and big.
They don't scare me.
Even if they crawl or
Even bite me.
I'm still OK.

I'm not scared,
Even if mythical creatures
Burn the horizon.
Even if it is a nightmare,
I think it's real.

Even if I shout,
Or even yell,
It's not because
I'm scared,
It's because I'm all alone.

Dreams are better than nightmares,
But they never come.
I'm not scared.
I just want to wake up from
This never-ending nightmare.

Robert Markley (15)
William Bradford Community College

My Life

I walk on stage
All I see of the audience is darkness
I feel the boards of the stage underneath me
I lower my head
I lower my body
I feel the hot rays of the theatre lights pierce into my skin.

It begins
I can feel two thousand pairs of eyes carefully watching me
I dance
I become one with the music, the theatre
I think of nothing else
Only focused on the performance
I feel free
I feel alive

It finishes
Silence
Then, the theatre bursts into applause
I glow
I realise . . . this is my life . . .

Adele Taylor (14)
William Bradford Community College

They Call Him The 'Geek'

Look at him over there,
The 'geek', they call him, with the weirdo hair,
He looks at me with hope in his eyes,
That one day I'll take his side.

According to them he's a waste of time,
At the end of the day,
He's not the one wasting his life,
Smoke;
Drink;
Drugs.

They accept me for being me,
And not following their pointless life,
So what's the difference between him and me?
I don't know, ask them not me!

Natasha Talbott (15)
William Bradford Community College

Footy Madness

Whatever you call it, football or soccer,
    just listen to this and I'll tell you a whopper.
Twenty-two men all trying to score,
    whilst listening to the crowd roar.
A ref with a whistle just waiting to blow,
    the player with the ball just trying to flow.
The man in the area just waiting to shoot,
    he must connect with his leather boot.
The player shoots, he hits the bar,
    the keeper collects and says, 'Thanks, ta.'
In football there are plenty of fouls,
    but most of the time the problem's the crowd.
The game is so great played all over the country,
    the trophies you win, the best in the century.
The crowd in the stand is all very wired,
    as the game draws to an end, the players are all tired.

Christopher Gutteridge (14)
William Bradford Community College

Visiting

Going to visit my uncle,
At his own home.
It's great to see him,
I don't even moan.

It's something I do every week,
Usually I don't do things I have to do,
But this,
I really love to do.

Then one week I didn't go.
That week didn't seem right.
I felt sad and angry,
But I didn't put up a fight.

The next week I went again,
But not to his home.
I felt strange at this place,
Like I wasn't on my own.

Most people were carrying flowers,
I was as well.
People laid them on the ground.
Each having a story to tell.

I laid my flowers by the pool,
There were a few flowers there.
I stood and looked around,
And then I felt scared.

I sat down and tears filled my eyes,
I realised why I was there.
I still visit him now,
But at the place that people share.

Hannah Maydwell (15)
William Bradford Community College

Death Row

The building is dark,
every weekend a million sparks.
They say a scream can be heard a mile away,
so many men killed each day.
The executioner is tall and tough,
he is bald and quite rough.
The prisoners will always pray,
as they lie there waiting for that day.
To sit in the chair and bear the pain,
but they have to play in the game.
They killed people in their lives,
and now it's time to sit and cry.
The families shall laugh at the brutal execution,
that the murderer will pay for what he's done.
They will drift away to Hell,
for another killer to wait in the cell.

Kevin Szymkowiak (14)
William Bradford Community College

I Have A Thing . . .

I have a thing I use a lot
I use it every day,
Most of the time it lies forgot
It has nothing to say.

We take this thing for granted
It can make a funny noise,
No one ever thanks it
Inside it's very moist.

I nibble this thing every day
I always take it to school,
If I forget it, there's a delay
And I look a fool.

'What is this thing?' I hear you say,
It is a *pen! Way-hey!*

Rachel Scattergood (14)
William Bradford Community College

I Am A Prisoner

My house is like a prison,
I'm always stuck in here,
I don't know how I'm living
My folks don't even care.

Every day I try,
To leave the house for good,
If only, if only,
If only I could.

I really love my parents
But I think they hate me,
I wish there wasn't an atmosphere,
If only they could see.

What I did was wrong
I know that now for sure
What is it that I can do
To find that simple cure?

My house is like a prison,
I'm always stuck in here,
I don't know how I'm living
My folks don't even care.

Amy Cotterill (14)
William Bradford Community College

Death

I've been shot in the head,
When I woke up, I was dead.
In a lift to Heaven to see Saint Peter,
I asked to enter, he said ,'*No!*'
Falling down 10,000 feet,
Don't know where I'm going
Or whom I'll meet,
The ground is coming.
Closer, closer, closer, *bang!*

I must be a cat, I landed on my feet,
Who's walking to me?
He's laughing at me,
He's beckoning me,
He's taunting me,
He offers me a fag
And takes it away,
He calls me 'gay',
He tells me what to do,
I follow what he says.

He tells me what I want to hear,
He pushes a button and *whoosh!*
Flying up, up, up and up until *boom!*

I can see a white light,
A man over me
'Am I dead?' I asked
'No, you're alive but you did pass away for a few weeks.'

David Rostron-Edwards (15)
William Bradford Community College

Holidays

Holidays are the best
With sand, sea and sun
When the plane lands
The fun begins

Everything feels so good
Everybody is relaxed
You want it never to end

Sitting by the pool
Nothing seems to matter
Everything is calm

But then it ends
You feel so bad
You wish you had done things
That you didn't
But then you think that
It won't be long before
You're back again.

Philip Parkes (14)
William Bradford Community College

What If?

What if,
There were no birds in the sky,
No fish in the sea,
No animals at all,
Where could they be?

What if,
There was no music to listen to,
And no PS2,
No TV or mobile,
What would we do?

What if,
There was no way to travel,
Nothing to drive, fly or sail,
No computer or Internet,
Would that mean no e-mail?

What if,
There was no home to go to,
And no love to give,
No one to help us,
Would we live?

What if,
There was no God,
And nobody to care,
No Heaven or Hell,
What is out there?

What if,
There was nothing whatsoever,
No land and no sea,
No world . . .
Where would we be?

Amy Fife (14)
William Bradford Community College

World War I!

I really hate the trenches,
So uncomfortable and small,
There should be at least some benches,
It feels smaller than my hall!
It's dirty and the smell is so foul,
Rotting bodies getting eaten by rats,
It smells like something left by a cow,
I can't wait to get home and read the welcome sign on my doormat.
My feet are so fat and sore,
Fear of death and fear of falling,
But the commander keeps telling me to go back for more,
I hate to have to keep on crawling!
My wife knows the chance of me returning is slim,
I keep getting wet and cold,
I'm surprised I've not lost a limb,
I feel really old.
We all have trench foot,
We are surrounded by lice,
But all the general says is, 'Keep your mouth shut!'
I'm so hungry I might start to eat the mice.
I'm going to carry on praying for an end,
But I'll keep trying to be strong,
Because I'm sick of giving the trenches a mend,
Even if I do it all wrong!

Rose Hopewell (14)
William Bradford Community College

All In Your Head

Whispered words chase you everywhere,
As you walk past.
Vicious words sometimes thrown, but
You just ignore them.

Old friends have turned their backs,
'We don't know that liar,' they claim.
No one argues, although they know it's true
That you used to be best mates.

No one believed you, thought you'd lied,
When you told your story.
Now they say you're crazy,
Always trying to bring you down.

'That would never happen,' you hear them declare,
'It's all just in your head.'
But deep inside - you know the truth,
It's not pretend, it really happened.

But you begin to doubt yourself -
You start to lose your mind.
Was it really real? you think
Or is it all in my head?

Jess Wright (15)
William Bradford Community College

Why Me?

As I'm sitting here,
Crying out my final tear,
I think to myself . . . *why me?*

Why give me the evil eye
Every time I came your way?
Why did you think I was
The one that had to pay?
Why push me to the ground
And get all your clones to laugh at me?
All I ever wanted was to be normal, to be free.

So as I'm sitting here,
Crying out my final tear,
I think to myself . . . *why me?*

Emily Blowers (15)
William Bradford Community College

Would I Run . . . ?

As I lie in these trenches,
All covered in mud,
I can't help but wonder,
Would I run if I could?

Would I fight for my country?
Would I die in the Somme?
Would I bleed all alone
Like I saw my mate, Tom?

As I lie in these trenches,
Shells explode all around,
Gunfire never ceases,
My face hits the ground.

The order is screamed,
'Men over the top.'
My head says, 'Just obey!'
My heart says, *'No, stop!''*

As I lie in these trenches,
To home my thoughts turn
My wife, my kids, my real life,
For these things I yearn.

I've seen battles in this war,
Some lost and some won,
Lost mates I've come to love,
With one shot of a gun.

As I lie in these trenches,
Orders ringing in my ear.
I wonder will I have made a difference
In this war, this time next year.

As I lie in these trenches,
All covered in mud,
I couldn't help but wonder,
Would I run if I could?

Jordan Woodward (14)
William Bradford Community College

Autumn

As crispy leaves fall to the ground,
the wind gushes around, making a swirling sound.
As the branches in the trees howl and wave,
the tide in the sea roars in the cave.
As footsteps crunch on the dead leaves and stones,
in the distance, far away, a lonely swing creaks and moans.

Naomi Sands (14)
William Bradford Community College

Late Again

Late again,
Passengers waiting for their train
The train and its coaches snake along the track
If it doesn't arrive soon, my boss will give me the sack.

Late again,
This time, stuck behind a freight train
Will I ever get to work?
The carriages sway and jerk.

Late again,
Where's the train?
Standing on the station
Always late to my occupation.

Late again,
Are they still using a steam train?
'Delayed,' the announcer says
This is the curse of Britain's railways.

Richard Armstrong (14)
William Bradford Community College

Football Crazy

As the whistle blows, the game begins
The ball flies around, the players chasing
Five minutes gone, a crunching tackle, we're through!
One on one, goalie versus forward
The tension builds as the goalie narrows the angle
The forward gets ready to shoot
He releases the ball, it rises over the goalie
It keeps rising, the forward looks nervous
It hits the underside of the crossbar, and it's in!
The crowd cheers and it's 1-0
The game restarts
Not long left in the first half
The ball is played into the middle
A long shot
Hits the post, so close
The half-time whistle blows.

The teams are back out, and the game restarts
A long ball over, the goalie comes out
He trips the player, penalty!
The player puts the ball down
The ref blows, the player starts his run
He shoots, wide
Two minutes left
A long shot! It's two-nil, the ref blows the whistle
They've won!

Jonathon Fields (15)
William Bradford Community College

Love!

Love is a gift,
Which doesn't come cheap,
Love is an ambition,
Which seems impossible to reach,
Love is an angel,
Sent from above,
Love clings to pairs,
Like socks or gloves,
Love is a taste,
Either bitter or sweet,
Love is that person,
You're longing to meet,
Love is a committed part of life,
Which can become more,
Like man and wife,
Love is so precious,
So keep it safe,
Love can be snatched,
At any time and any place,
Love is that thing,
You're desperate to find,
Love is unnoticed,
Striking you blind,
Love is a key,
A key to your heart,
So when that loved one
Has been found,
Don't let them depart!

Lisa Betteridge (14)
William Bradford Community College

Where Has All The Love Gone?

Where has all the love gone?
Nobody seems to care.
All the marriages breaking up,
What a life of despair!
People not caring how their children
Feel being torn between the two,
Wondering which one has made this happen,
Which one they should choose.
We need to make this a life of peace
Not tearing people to discover,
There's nothing in their life for them,
Nothing to make them care.
So let's not do this to the world
Not make them feel in despair.

Jodie Turner (14)
William Bradford Community College

Bikes

Bikes are the best
They go with a zest
You sit on the seat
And feel the heat
If you've got the bottle
You can pull back the throttle
Zip up your pocket
You'll go like a rocket

As the wheels go round
They stick to the ground
Going up a gear
You increase the fear
You come to a stop
And your ears go *pop!*

Luke Horton-Walker (14)
William Bradford Community College

England Vs Argentina

Wasn't the best match in the world
A bit of a boring game
Quite a few chances
Very end-to-end stuff

I was sitting on the sofa
At my nanna's house
My dad was there too
We were watching the game

Half-time arrived
The two coaches rung up the changes
Seventeen passes without losing the ball
Pretty good - eh?

We were playing well
But so were they
They brought Batistuta on for a bit of flair
Didn't really work though

Beckham was looking forward to this match
After his sending off in the '98 World Cup
It was against Argentina
Simeone, an Argentinean player, provoked him, of course

Suddenly, Owen was tripped in the box
No question who would take it if it were a penalty
Yesss! The ref blew his whistle
It was a penalty!

At last, something actually happened
Simeone whispered in Beckham's ear
Every English fan on the edge of their seat
Beckham stepped up to take it
He took a deep breath
Bottom left corner, he'd scored and we had won the game, *yesss!*

Shaun Curtis (14)
William Bradford Community College

Where Has Our Love Gone?

At the start you gave me your heart,
We never walked alone or far part,
We said we'd always be forever,
They said we belonged together,
You used to tell me everything,
Now all I get is a little wink,
Yeah, you make me smile,
But this feeling I have is so fragile,
I have nothing left of me and you,
Just some memories, but only a few,

Where has it gone?
Where is our love that we had for so long?

It's drifted off and vanished,
As though someone had it banished,
It's gone from our heart,
It's gone from our head,
I knew it would only take time until our love was dead.

Where has it gone?
Where is our love that we had for so long?

Rebecca Clarke (14)
William Bradford Community College

The Two Hunters

You cannot see me
I stalk your shadow
You check behind
And scan the plateau

You feel scared
You begin to sweat
Now your fear is declared
Coming here you regret

You look left and right
You know I am there
It's the middle of the night
I can taste your despair

I bide my time
For the sheer thrill
It will not be long now
Till I go for the kill

I take my chance
I pounce on your back
But you are too quick
You are prepared for attack

I land and turn around
You are fast to aim your gun
My loud roar is drowned
By the shot from your weapon

Now I go to your market
Sold for useless goods
An expensive coat maybe
Or poor coating for woods

Although my body is now gone
My proud spirit will forever live on.

Richard Dawson (15)
William Bradford Community College

Trying To Save I Love You . . .

I have known you for so long
And my feelings keep getting strong
I thought I loved you as a friend
But then I realised my love for you would never end
I used to let you see me cry
But now when you talk to me I go all shy
I'm scared to tell you how I feel
In case I lose you for real
I think about you night and day
And I dream that you're mine and you'll always stay
If only that was true
You'd see how much I love you.
I wish you'd take me in your arms and say,
That you feel the same way.
Just remember whatever you do,
I will always love you.

Laura Gould (14)
William Bradford Community College

Animals

A nimals are the ones being hunted,
N ever the hunter always the hunted,
I nvestigators looking for the killers,
M an or is it another crook?
A nimals are being hunted for coats or ivory,
L ooking for a place to hide,
S lowly slipping into slumber.

Liam Bailey (14)
William Bradford Community College

Summer Days

The cool summer breeze,
Blowing through the sand dunes,
Making the sea grass chatter,
Warm smells filling the air.

Heads of sun-bleached waves bobbing through the crowds,
The sand, silky-smooth, as it passes through your toes,
And in the distant, summer's tunes can be heard from a radio.

It's getting cooler now,
New smells start to fill the air,
Barbecues!

The aroma drifting in clouds hypnotising people,
Making them wander in hoards towards it.

Now it's night and everyone's huddled around a fire,
Sitting in the bay,
Waiting for the next summer day.

Melissa Forman (14)
William Bradford Community College

Summer Days!

Sun, warmth, breeze,
Ice cream, pop, sweets,
Bikini, hot pants, shorts,
T-shirt, cap and more.

Sea, beach, sand,
Swim, run, land,
Sunbathe, relax, enjoy,
With all your girls and boys!

Smile, smirk and laugh,
Be happy and don't be daft,
Don't stand all day and gaze,
Enjoy the summer days!

Chantelle Osborne (14)
William Bradford Community College

Another Day

I walked into the playground,
And looked around to see,
Everybody staring,
Laughing at me.

I just ignore them,
What is the point?
I carried on walking,
I didn't look at them.

They try to get inside my head,
But it never works.
But today it was different,
It began to hurt.

I got into school,
It carried on there,
They look like zombies,
All they do is stare.

I thought for a while,
What shall I do?
Should I tell a teacher
And get my head shoved down the loo?

I thought I'd try a tactic,
One I haven't tried.
I'll try to beat the bullies but still stay kind.

They know I've had enough now,
And they've run out of jokes,
I'll start another day again,
This time without the pokes.

Amy Fowler (14)
William Bradford Community College

Every Day

I've been on a merry-go-round for as long as I can remember,
The same things happen, it makes me tremble,
The days drag on and the time moves slow,
The clouds whiz by, just one minute to go,
There she is, built like a double-decker bus,
I will walk home quietly without a fuss,
The bell starts to ring and everyone runs out,
There she is, she charges at me like a bull,
She goes to hit me but hits a displayed skull,
As I run home the cars fly by,
Tomorrow it will be the same, I give a big sigh.

Kirstie Hewitt (14)
William Bradford Community College

Tick-Tock

Tick-tock
went the clock
another minute passed.
The hands of time move on and on
and before you know it you have gone,
so make the most of the time you have
because time ticks on
and then you are gone.

Sarah Collins (14)
William Bradford Community College

Life

Life is so fast,
It moves like the wind,
Love comes and goes,
So quickly you don't realise.

Special people are always there,
They beat like a heart,
Friends move on and leave you,
Whatever happens, there's someone
Who is always there!

Alisia Evans (14)
William Bradford Community College

The Great Big Oak Tree

The great big oak tree,
Swaying in the wind.
Standing tall, much bigger than me,
And the birds chirping in the breeze.

The great big oak tree,
How I'd longed to climb it.
Up I went, scraping my knee,
But still I went on bit by bit.

The great big oak tree,
Birds scattering as I did go.
I sat there watching a bee,
But still I didn't know,
How high I'd gone until I fell.

The great big oak tree,
Swaying innocently in the wind.
When I returned there with
A cast around my knee.

Ben Carroll (14)
William Bradford Community College

Time Is Moving

Time is moving
Ticking away
No time left
So much to do and say,

Time is moving
Right here, right now
Must do what we want
Before time runs out.

Time is moving
What do we do?
Make friends, break friends
Find those that are true.

Time has gone
Are you too late?
Live life to the full
Don't leave it to fate.

Alanna Kavanagh (14)
William Bradford Community College

Finding The Sea

Flowing waters, cool and deep,
lapping waves or calming sleep.
Down the valley, through the stream,
to find the sea: a river's dream.

Crystal waters, rush downhill,
cloudy mist and winter chill.
Over pebbles, through the stream,
to find the sea: a river's dream.

Across the valley meadowlands,
down the hillsides, through the sands.
Over seashells, past the stream,
it's found the sea, and met its dream.

Kim Fawcett (15)
William Bradford Community College

Electricity

Taken for granted,
it's just there,
beating, pulsing, racing.

We use it day and night,
and don't even care,
moving, flashing, sparking.

But what would we do
if it wasn't there?
Would we survive
and would we care?
Beating, pulsing, racing.

We would not survive,
and have to care,
for our surroundings
and we would share,
moving, flashing, sparking.

Taken for granted,
it's just there,
beating,
pulsing,
racing.

We use it day and night,
and don't even care,
moving,
flashing,
sparking.

Jaeven Bradbury (14)
William Bradford Community College

The Stars

Stars, beautiful, shiny stars
Up there glistening in the dark ocean of black
With the moon, the biggest, brightest star in the sky
Little tiny dots surrounding the moon
I look out of my window, with the stars lighting up my room
Soon it will be dawn
And the sun comes up and the stars disappear
The stars still there, waiting for the moon and the dark sky
The sun still up there, taking over the moon
The rays of light beating down on the Earth
But suddenly the sun starts to move
Disappearing on the other side of the Earth
The first star I see
Then a few more
Till all the stars are up
But the moon, not as bright as the stars
Only half of it to be seen
The moon is not as perfect as the stars.

Lucy Bates (14)
William Bradford Community College

What Is Time . . .

Time is . . .
Always changing things,
The latest look in fashion,
Your best friend or your newest love.
It never stays the same,
And you're just expected to keep up.

Time is . . .
Getting you into sticky situations.
Persuading your mum to let you have a bit more of it,
Being late because you lost track of it,
Looking bored because you have too much of it.

Time is . . .
Letting things heal,
Whether it's a broken leg or a broken heart.
Trying to patch things up,
Waiting for enough to pass and making that decision.

Time is . . .
Never letting you have it easy.
It never lets you get away with anything,
That late piece of homework,
That rumour you thought would pass
Or the two minutes difference arriving late or on time.

Time is . . .
Something you can't escape,
Always there like a shadow.
Sometimes it helps or aggravates you.
But no one knows what it can bring and maybe take with it!

Sarah Battle (14)
William Bradford Community College

Time

Time can pass slowly,
Crawling like a tortoise,
Or it can speed up,
Running like a greyhound,
Sometimes it feels like time's standing still,
Like waiting in a traffic jam,
But at times it flies by,
Like a speed train,
It's funny!
Time flies when you're having fun,
But when you're bored, it drags on . . .
And on and on!

Emma Goldsberry (14)
William Bradford Community College

My Thumb

Explain away
When you say
I scribble away,
I try to make it go away
But it gets carried away,
Scribble, scribble, goes my thumb
He thinks that he is my mum
Scribbles, scribbles, everywhere
Goes my thumb without a care.

Charlotte Harbottle (14)
William Bradford Community College

Death

People say that life is better than death,
But I tend to disagree
With all the troubles that life throws at us,
Surely death is easier for you and me?
Though when death is upon us,
The decision is to be made,
Heaven or Hell?
It is your life,
Your choice must be made,
Heaven with the angels,
In the clouds on high,
Or Hell with the Devil,
The burning fire.
Choose how you will,
Choose how you want,
But in the end your afterlife is left to *fate!*

Gail L Brown (14)
William Bradford Community College

The Batsmen

The batsman stands at the crease
like a warrior waiting for battle.
His padding like the armour worn
by knights in the medieval times.

He looks round the field, his battleground,
as the bowler positions his field
like a general organising his foot soldiers.

The batsman, armed with his bat,
his lance, his weapon and shield
not only to score the runs
but to defend himself from the ball
as it is fired at him at 100mph
like the ball from a cannon.

The batsman stays in, ball after ball,
focused, blacking out the wicket keeper
cracking jokes like a jester in a king's court.

A good over, the batsman smacks
two fours and a six showing the bowler
who's 'boss', like a lion laying
down his territory, showing a message
to all those fielders.

The next ball is bowled, a touch
of the bat and into the gloves,
'Howzat?' a loud shout from all the fielders
like a battle cry and the umpire signals,
                                        Out!

Danni Smart (14)
William Bradford Community College

My Ghost

Here I sit
Alone in this room,
Staring into space.
Slowly it moves
The shadow in this room.
A slight breeze follows
Sending shivers up my spine.

It's scary up here alone
In an unknown surrounding
Nothing to be seen . . .
Nothing to be known,
Just, a ghost!

A ghost with no surrounding
A ghost of whom no one knows
A ghost with no name
Just, a ghost of which I only know.

Claire Miles (14)
William Bradford Community College

Trapped

Looking from the inside,
Always looking out,
I'm looking through the window,
Now I have no doubt.
This must be the sign,
Because I can't get through the door,
I can't find a key,
I can't be bothered anymore.

I still sit in my room,
And stare towards the sky,
Watching other people,
As their time goes by.
No one seems to notice me,
As I sit here alone,
Looking for the key of life,
But all I find is a knife.

Jodie Smith (14)
William Bradford Community College

I, The Wind

I, the wind, can be strong and steady,
Or I can whip you off your feet when you're not ready.

I, the wind, am invisible to your eye,
You can only tell I'm near when I'm passing you by.

I, the wind, am destructive and gentle,
I push trees into road or play against your face when
                                     the sun is mental.

I, the wind, can be still as night,
Can be silent as a thief or as brutal as a knight.

I, the wind, can be a useful friend,
But only if you take care of the world to the very end.

I, the wind, am an element, a source,
I can give you power then take everything with force.

I am, after all, the *wind!*

Louise Cooper (14)
William Bradford Community College

A Dog . . .

A dog is a man's best friend,
who will stay with you 'til the end.

It fetches sticks,
eats bones and does tricks.

If you let it sit on your lap,
or lie in front of the fire on the mat.

It may bark, or be quiet,
no other animal is like it.

It will not betray you,
it will stand by your side and love you.

It keeps you company when you are down,
its big ears makes it look like a clown.

A dog is a man's best friend,
who will stay with you till the end.

Lucy Pratt (15)
William Bradford Community College

Gone

An empty space deep inside,
The pain within I cannot hide.
Images of you flash through my mind,
The strength to stand, I cannot find.
I long for you to walk through the door,
I long to see your face once more.
Your bright wide eyes, a happy smile,
Wish I could be with you, for just a while.
The minutes turn to hours as I sit and think of you,
The times we spent together, days apart were few.
The tears I have cried, smiles I have none,
I love you more now you're . . . *gone!*

Stacey Bridge (14)
William Bradford Community College

I See England

I look through a blue window,
I see peace,
I see happiness,
I see beauty,
I see England!

I turn my head, to the red window,
I see war,
I see crime,
I see destruction,
I see England!

I put my ear to the blue wall,
I hear laughter,
I hear birds singing,
I hear England!

I put my ear on the red wall,
I hear crying,
I hear screaming,
I hear England!

Which is real . . .
Red?
Blue?
White?

Jack Jordan (14)
William Bradford Community College

Friends

Friends are like cushions,
as they are there to comfort you.
Friends are like the sun,
as they can brighten the darkest day.
Friends are like presents,
as they can surprise you in many ways.
Friends are like diaries,
as you can trust them with your deepest fears and secrets.
Friends are like holidays,
as they are full of excitement and fun.
Friends are like the most precious gift,
as you should treasure them with your heart,
and never let anything come between you.

Laura Davies (14)
William Bradford Community College

Vampire

In the woods he stalks his prey,
his cold, dark eyes, small and grey.
Through the trees, over the hill,
the night is silent, calm and still.
His hearing is keen, his breathing steady,
his long white fangs, sharp and ready.
He sees his victim, he's quick, he's fast,
through the leaves and then, at last,
he tastes its fear and feels its pain
as it struggles to get away in vain.

Marie Johnson (14)
William Bradford Community College

Mum

Mum can be nice,
She loves a slice of the action,
So be careful,
You have to dareful,
To argue your point,
She thinks she know what is best for me,
But I have to say I don't always agree,
If I wear high heels
She says they'll damage my back,
But if I don't, my friends will think I'm slack,
So what do I do in this world of confusion?
Do I listen to her and get called a geek
Or do I follow the herd and become a sheep?
I could hang out with thugs,
I could even take drugs,
But at the end of the day who are the mugs?
She has seen it before
And as I walk out the door,
She says, 'Whatever you do,
I will always love you.'
It's best to be really strong inside,
Then when faced with choices, I could decide.

Annabel Baxter (14)
William Bradford Community College

The Bully

He hides in the toilet,
He thinks I cannot see,
He sits in the cubicle,
He tries to avoid me.

I kick open the door,
It hits the wall with a bang,
As I hit him, his glasses
Hit the floor with a *clang*.

I can see he's helpless,
I know this is wrong,
But I cannot stop myself,
I feel like a god.

I leave him lying there,
I turn and walk away,
I act like I don't care,
But deep down I'm as hurt as him.

Now I hear he's gone away,
I've nothing much to do,
But I vow that he will pay,
But I am paying more.

He's gone away forever,
He's dead and it's all my fault,
I shouldn't have hit him so hard,
Then he wouldn't have used that rope.

The kids at school don't cheer me on,
They turn and hiss and spit,
Now I know that I was wrong,
But now it's all too late!

Sarah Telford (14)
William Bradford Community College

On Your Marks!

The athlete drops into his blocks,
He focuses on his goal.
He looks down, then up at the finish.
The starter calls,
'Get set!'
His pulse is racing, anticipating the gun.
The crowd falls silent, waiting for the
Bang!
The gun goes,
He's out of his blocks,
He's getting into his stride.
He no longer feels his beating heart.
He's over the finish line,
What a run!
It's a photo finish
But, has he won?

Steven Barnes (14)
William Bradford Community College

The Wind In The Trees

The wind was howling through the trees.
The branches were rattling and rustling.
The tiles on the roof were falling off
And the people were screaming.

People were running in every direction.
Panicking, screaming and yelling.
The wind was howling through the street
And sweeping people up off their feet.

They were being carried for miles at a time.
Suddenly stopping, then starting again.
They were twirling round and round,
Until the wind died down.

Ben Leadbetter (14)
William Bradford Community College

Alone

I could hear the train coming
The lines trembled beneath my feet
But still the bullies held me back
Stopped me getting to safety.

First I tried to fight
But I failed miserably
There were just too many
And I was just too weak.

So I pleaded with them to let me off the tracks,
But just as I feared, they laughed,
Told me I was a fool,
I started to believe them, although
I knew they were just being cruel.

I cried out for help, from the people all around
But they tried hard not to notice I'd fallen to the ground.
The train was getting closer, beginning to grow in size.

As the train came closer,
Their laughter died away.
These bullies, they all scattered
Fearing for themselves.
I was left alone, no one by my side,
What wouldn't I give for one friendly last goodbye.

Ellie Carr (14)
William Bradford Community College

Time Passing By

I wake up in the morning,
At the break of every day,
I can hear my clock ticking,
While in my bed I lay.
I think about my life,
And wonder if and why?
I worry about what I'm going to do,
While the time is passing by.

I drag myself out of bed,
And wonder about the day ahead.
I can still hear my clock,
Its loud tick-tock, tick-tock.
I stop, look, think and sigh,
As I worry about how fast,
The time is whizzing by.

Everything around me,
Is busy as we speak.
Including the time passing,
A hour, a day, a week.
As I go about my chores,
I look out from my eye,
And see the whole world busy,
As the time is rushing by.

Finally the day is done,
And again it's time to rest.
Today has gone quickly,
Tomorrow will seem even less.
I hurry to my bed,
Close my eyes and sigh,
As I reflect on my day,
That has already passed by.

Charlotte Russell (14)
William Bradford Community College

Stars, Stars, Stars

Stars, stars, stars,
They're moving slowly across the moor
In the sky as the dark appears and the day disappears
The stars twinkle just like your eyes twinkle during the day
They twinkle brightly at night, in the sky as they sit nearby
The moon goes down with the stars at night.
They slip silently away in the morning as we wake up.
We normally spend hours looking at them
And we can't stop looking at them
Because they twinkle bright at night.
They hide during the day.
With the moon behind the moors, it sleeps alone
Till night appears again and they come out and twinkle brightly.

Katie Robinson (14)
William Bradford Community College

Time Flies By When You're Having Fun

When I'm at the park playing football
it seems like I've been playing for ten minutes
and I've been playing for an hour
and it's time to go home.

When I get home and I get back late
I only get there at twenty past eight.
I go to a party and it's over in a flash,
but I know I've had one hell of a laugh.

When it finally gets to Christmas Day
the day's almost over and you've nothing to say.
But when you die of old age
time flies by, time flies by.

Gordon Kings (14)
William Bradford Community College

The Seasons

Springtime is almost here,
It's nearly that special time of year,
Bulbs are coming through the ground,
Elegance will soon be all around,
As I walk across the ground,
Beautiful colours will be found.

Summertime is lots of sun,
We all love to have such fun,
Through the fields we love to run,
Bright and light summer nights,
The stars sparkle in the sky,
Hazy, lazy summer nights,
Make me feel all warm inside.

Autumn leaves fall to the ground,
And yet they don't make a sound,
Shadows of the big bare tree,
Look so scary at night to me,
Autumn winds cut through me and you,
And are telling us that winter is nearly due.

Wintertime and the snow is falling,
I hear the robin softly calling,
He's sitting on my window ledge,
I'm wishing I were on my sledge,
But sadly I have a cold,
So off to bed I go instead.

Cheryl White (14)
William Bradford Community College

You're The One

We've known each other for so many years,
We've shared the laughter, we've shared the tears.
We've even had our ups and downs,
But true friends will always be around.

We've known each other for so long,
I never thought you'd do anything wrong
Then I found this wasn't true,
And I found out that I loved you.

All I could do was gaze in your eyes,
But love was what you didn't realise.
When I thought of you I just floated,
Now my heart is totally devoted.

Then I saw that you loved me,
It was a thing I never thought could be.
Together we spent so much quality time,
Nothing could split us, not even crime.

Now I'm scared you're going to say,
It's not working, we're drifting away,
Even if we do split apart,
You will always remain deep in my heart.

Now that I am not with you,
I don't know what I'm going to do,
Maybe it's because we've known each other for years,
Going out at night and drinking beers.

Now in my heart lies a very black hole,
Your heart must be black, like a lump of coal.
Now there is one thing that I can see,
What I thought was love, wasn't meant to be.

But one thing I know is now you're gone
I truly know that you are the one.

Jennie Wall (14)
William Bradford Community College

Golden Autumn

Autumn's golden sunshine bright,
Dancing shadows, dark and light;
Colours brown, green, orange and yellow,
Wind is blowing, slight and mellow.
Squirrels settle over leaf-covered ground,
Can you hear the winter's sound?
Like music drifting in freshening air,
Wondrous colours make me stand and stare.
Rolling leaves on the ground at night,
Small little rodent caught in tawny owl's sight,
Flies from its perch to pounce on its prey,
Back to its nest to sleep through the day.
Dawn now has broken, the east is aglow,
Cool is the weather, there's a chance of some snow;

Warm-blooded animals hide in the ground,
Deep underground till the spring brings new sound.

Kerry Ekin (14)
William Bradford Community College

Peace?

As I gaze into the sky,
Watching the clouds float by,
I wonder what might be happening
On the other side of the world?

Is someone starving in Africa
Or fighting in the Far East?
What is there that I can do
To bring the world to peace?

A single person cannot bring peace alone,
But if we all work together, then the fighting
can be postponed.
So put down your guns,
And share your food because this way
the peace can be proved.

Laura Illstone   (14)
William Bradford Community College

The Day At The Races

I've put my bet, I want to win,
It's my favourite day, at the races.

They start, I'm number four, come on, come on!
They swap positions weaving in and out
After the rabbit who's going to win,
It is my favourite day at the races.

Yes, number four is in front, I'm going to win,
Miles in front of the others,
There are only inches to go,
Closer, closer,
Yes, I've won! I leap in joy!
It is my favourite day at the races.

Adam Taylor (14)
William Bradford Community College

Cricket Match

C is for concentration when playing
R is for runs, which help you to win the match
I is for winning the international World Cup
C is for catching the last man out
K is for killing the middle stump when bowling
E is for enjoying the game
T is for teamwork

M is for murdering the bad deliveries when batting
A is for attacking bowling
T is for testing bowling outside the off-stump
C is for confidence when playing
H is for hitting a '6' out of the ground!

David Nicholson (14)
William Bradford Community College

Mum

Mum's the world to me
She even cooks my tea
And cleans my clothes
And she cares for me.

Mum's the world to me
She's my advisor
And my best mate
And she cares for me.

Mum's the world to me
She's always there
And we get along
And she cares for me
And she cares for me.

Kimberly Remmer (14)
William Bradford Community College

Eyes

They give you a wink,
They can twinkle like stars,
They can belong to a person,
Who sends you to Mars,
They might be your friends,
Or someone you know,
But for some reason,
That's where things show,
Like love and hate,
Happiness and despair,
But whatever it is,
You will always care,
About the way they look,
Or see through your heart,
You know you're in love,
Right from the start,
Sometimes it's different,
And the look is like sin,
There's something between you,
That hurts from within,
Puppy-dog eyes,
They're hard to explain,
They look sweet and innocent,
But may cover up pain,
Yet, eyes are like diamonds,
All crystal clear,
You can see straight through them,
Whether you're far or near.

Siouxie Ovington (14)
William Bradford Community College

Image

I was walking down the road one day
Just staring at my feet
When a girl who looked around my age
Brushed past me on the street.
Her make-up was done perfectly
And she was really pretty and slim
Not a single hair was out of place
And her clothes were really 'in.'

Then as I passed a shop window
I saw the reflection of myself:
My messy hair, unfashionable clothes,
My tummy straining my sister's belt.

Some boys the girl knew came up to her
As she clumsily dropped her bag
She yelled at the lads 'Well . . . pick it up!'
She seemed like such a drag.
While walking past a busy stall
She knocked over some merchandise
And didn't even go back to help
Or stop to apologise.

When I first saw that girl and then saw me
I was so down, I nearly cried
But now I look at me and think to myself
'Well at least I have beauty inside!'

Emma Gracias (14)
William Bradford Community College

Football Match

F is for frantic clearance as their striker makes an early appearance
O is for on the attack, their players struggling to get back
O is for on side. It's a *goal!* The early attacks took its toll
T is for two-nil. A shot from near the 'penno' spot
B is for bad luck, one of our players is in the book. Free kick
A is for almost they have hit the post
L is for late celebration for them, they scored a conciliation
L is for last seconds that passed. We won 2-1.

M is for man of the match, for the best player out of the batch
A is for away win and that's not a sin
T is for terrific, we're still plerific
C is for all the claps from all the supporting chaps
H is for an hour and a half of a *football match!*

Lee Skene (14)
William Bradford Community College

Moving House

We drove down a road
Where I'd never been before
My mum stopped the car
There, for the first time I saw.

Before I knew where I was
There was a sign outside the door
Next day strangers came to visit
So I hid behind the door.

Soon boxes littered my house
Stress levels began to rise
Then one day someone said,
'This house is no longer yours!'

All the boxes then disappeared
So did my bed and clothes
Then I was driven down the road
Where we parked outside a house.

The first week was hectic
With people in and out
But now I finally realise
What all the fuss was about!

Faye Millington (15)
William Bradford Community College

Holidays

H ot sand under your feet,
O cean waves are roaring,
L icking ice lollies and eating sweets,
I n the heat of the morning,
D eckchairs by the poolside,
A ll day spent making sandcastles,
Y es, and on the dodgem rides,
S uper holidays away from hassle.

Shanie Evans (15)
William Bradford Community College

Friendship

F riends are loyal
R eliable
I nteresting and great to be with
E specially kind
N ice to you
D ear to the heart
S incere
H elpful
I deal to keep you laughing when you're down.
P robably the only friend you will ever care for.

Katy McSporran (14)
William Bradford Community College

Classroom

Boring teacher babbling on,
Children wishing they were gone,
Wishing they were in some other place,
Instead of in front of the teacher's face.

I look up at the clock,
Is it me or has it stopped?
My eyes are glazed over, I am so bored,
All I am thinking is, *save me, Lord.*

Time ticks on, it's time to go but he keeps us behind,
Can't he see the clock, is he blind?
I want to go now before it gets too late,
I just can't wait to walk out of the school gate.

Sam Yeomans (15)
William Bradford Community College

The Wind

The wind flows softly through the sky
Sweetly howling
Calmly floating way up high
Sweeping softly through the trees
Taking off all the leaves.

Suddenly the wind grows stronger
Forcefully whipping through the sky
These windy days are getting longer
Now the children play inside.

Kellie Roberts (14)
William Bradford Community College

Day After Day

As I wake, I find myself in the east,
Ready, waiting for another day of work.
I think to myself, *should I provide a nice day*
Which will please, or should I hide?

As the human race starts to emerge, I decide
To shine freely and to entertain,
Rather than be miserable and glum
And let it rain.

The children are playing beneath me and, in my presence,
Are running around, just like pheasants,
When they return to their homes, I have done,
My work is over so I set in the west.

Then my work begins again, day after day.

Abi Fowler (14)
William Bradford Community College

The Trees

They have a life of their own,
Moving and stretching.
As the winds of autumn graze through them,
The colours are magical.
The red and gold of the leaves
Swirling through the air as they fall.
Then just as they reach the ground,
The cool breeze sweeps them back up
So they can come whirling back through the atmosphere again.
As they fall,
The now bony fingers of the trees
Try to catch them.
The branches reach out
But miss.
Then the leaves slip softly to the ground
Where they stay.

Charlotte Bedford (14)
William Bradford Community College

Every Day

From day to day
Goes light and the night.

The clouds come out
To stop the sun from shining bright.
Grey or white, it's up to them
But when the sky goes dull
Beware, the rain will come.

Later in the day when it is going dark,
The moon will appear and show its face.
When dawn is on its way,
It will be repeated again.
It won't go away!

Time will keep on passing by.
This is recurring and will never die.

James Bone (14)
William Bradford Community College

Friends

F riends are always there
R eally kind, can be
I mmature, but very funny
E very friend you should treasure
N ever be
D isloyal as you can always lose them
S o keep them and treasure them always!

Natalie White (14)
William Bradford Community College

Night

The purity of day metamorphosing into the sweet lechery
of the night
The moon murders our sun
And in its death a world of fragile things has begun
We drown in its raptured twilight
The moon a crystal ball surrounded by claw-like clouds in
the abyss of the above
Each star like tears of tragedy engraved into the charred
canopy of black tranquillity
And in this tranquil sea of despair beings that were once
despised, wander under the mayhem of the immortal dark light,
swimming in the darkness without the criticism of the sun
Strange, however, that behind our cruel veil of judgement
we entrust all our dreams into the loving tender arms of the night,
yet we are afraid of this unknown beauty,
this goddess of translucent light
No matter how much we fear her, night will never abandon us
in its constant pursuit of the light
Dawn
Life and death embrace
The fire of the day brings the burden of living pandemonium
The nocturne of the shadow lost in its violating illusion
Yet we live on, moths to its flame
Until the moon conquers the sun.

Elena Hulme (14)
William Bradford Community College

Boys

Boys, boys, all types of boys,
Some boys are sweet, some boys are bad,
Some boys are weird, some boys get mad,
Boys, boys, all types of boys,
Some boys are rich, some boys are poor,
Some boys are exciting, some boys are a bore,
Boys, boys, all types of boys,
Some boys are quiet, some boys are loud,
Some boys are shy, some boys are proud,
Boys, boys, all types of boys,
Some boys are players, some boys are not,
Some boys are ugly, some boys are hot,
Boys, boys, all types of boys,
Some boys go out, some boys stay in,
Some boys are fat, some boys are thin,
Boys, boys, all types of boys,
Some boys love, and some boys lose,
But only the special boys are the ones
          I choose!

Sally Allen (14)
William Bradford Community College

Leicester City

They'll soon be going, going, gone
Back to Division One.
I suppose the Nationwide's not that bad
If I'm saying that I must be mad.

People saying, 'We'll never go down,' should just shut up!
Once they're down, they'll never come back up.
The fans shout, 'Come on Muzzy!'
Soon their vision of the Premiership will be fuzzy.

Soon they'll be in Division One
With the sight of the Premiership gone.
They'll say, 'How did it happen?' showing every
Leicester fan's a fool
Still they'll never again have to lose to Liverpool.

Jamie Clow (14)
William Bradford Community College

Night

Twinkling stars in the sky,
The day has passed by.
Inky blackness all around,
Ghostly shadows on the ground.

Cats stalk
Bats fly
The full moon is high

Wandering through the cold night air
Wide eyes stare . . .

Jessica Huckle (14)
William Bradford Community College

Guitars And Me

Les Paul, Gibson, Fender, Strat,
They're all great guitars and none sound flat,
The way I play, it feels to me, that I'm getting it down to a tee,
I like to play night and day, strum up and down, either way,
Sometimes I think I'm not that good, I will get better, I know I should,
I sit and think how good I should be,
But no one can beat the guitar and me,
We make a great team.

I do the strumming, it makes the sound,
The sound of this music, shakes through the ground,
People stand and watch, they may mock and laugh,
But no one can beat the guitar and me,
We make a great team.

Jamie Pratt (14)
William Bradford Community College

School

Most kids say that school is boring,
And in the lessons we are all yawning.
When it comes to the next school morning,
We wish we could carry on snoring.

Some kids say school is brill,
They say the lessons are a thrill.
But I think that school is OK,
Because I can chat to my mates all day.

Francesca Dolman (14)
William Bradford Community College

Funny

Isn't it funny when you can't think?
Think of a poem, your mind on the blink?
The words won't come into your head,
Your body awake but your mind in bed,
Then all of a sudden you get started,
And the pen and the paper cannot be parted.

Isn't it funny that I'm on the second verse now?
A revolution must have happened somehow.
Once I start, I cannot stop,
Writing and writing 'til my mind goes *pop!*
Now next time you don't know what to say,
Think of this and you'll be on your way.

Connie Overton (15)
William Bradford Community College

Queen Of Scum

Broken hearts
The queen of scum
What is this I have become?

Running from the truth
Escaping the lies
Fear and hope left in my eyes.

Engrave your name into my arm
Praying
You won't come to any harm.

Despising my memories
So few
Despise the way I've felt about you.

Hannah Brown (14)
William Bradford Community College

Lost

I ran away from home
It was midnight and I was alone
The howling winds of the midnight air
The feeling of fear I could not bear

The sound of an owl gave me a fright
I ran until I felt secure and alright
I felt like a shadow hanging over me
I felt anxious and also dreary

I was lost and surrounded by old, grazed trees
I wanted to arrive at a place where I felt at ease
Next it was morning, the sun was shimmering bright
The fear had disappeared, as it was daylight

Inside myself I convinced leaving home was wrong
But I was lost and the journey back home was long
I began my trip home
And soon I would not be alone

Finally I arrived home with faces of happiness surrounding me
My parents were especially pleased to see me
That night I went to bed
And woke up in the morning with a new day ahead.

Namita Mistry (14)
William Bradford Community College

My 13th Birthday

Up, up, up, away we go,
Over the hills far away.

My 13th birthday was such a treat,
I held on tight to my aeroplane seat.

To feel the freedom in the sky,
Like a bird away up high.

The sound of the engine, noisy and loud,
The sky blue above the cloud.

As I go on my way,
I will never forget this special day.

Grant Hubbard (14)
William Bradford Community College

A Football Story

Whether it's David Beckham or Ryan Giggs
Every player gives the same story

To be, and beat, the best
They all look for Championship glory

With his never-ending ego on the pitch
David Beckham makes the switch

From Man U to Real Madrid

He wishes he plays like George Best did . . .

Freddy Vesty (14)
William Bradford Community College

My Friends Are . . .

My friends are like angels,
Who always make me laugh.
When we go shopping,
Some of the clothes are naff.

My friends are like angels,
Without any wings.
We trust with all our heart,
With the most special things.

Emma Harris (14)
William Bradford Community College

Sunset

Look at the sunset setting in the sky,
Nobody notices, they just drive by.

The redness, purple, orange with blue,
Setting the scene for me and you.

After twenty minutes of going down,
Rising up in another town.

Now the night has drawn in,
The sun has come and has been.

As we snuggle in our bed,
Ready for the cold night ahead.

Jamie Slimm (14)
William Bradford Community College

You're So Lovely

You're so pretty
I'm singing this ditty
You're so lovely
And soft and cuddly

You're so smiley
I think of your laugh
You're like flowers
I think of you for hours

Lovely, lovely, lovely, oh
Lovely, lovely, oh

Why did you dump me?
I'm really sad
Text me or call me
It'll make me glad.

Samuel Oakes (14)
William Bradford Community College

Pushed To The Limit

He's dragging his feet,
He's hanging his head.
He sighs as he thinks,
Of the day ahead.

He enters the gate,
He hears the first shout.
Will somebody please
Come and help him out?

As he bites his lip,
Begins to wonder.
Could he end all this?
All day he ponders.

He heads for the bridge,
His mind is made up.
It's clear now that he jumps,
And clears this mess up.

He's over the rail,
He stares at the street.
Death's egging him on,
It's then their eyes meet.

He's jumped, he's falling,
He knows it's not far.
The sorrow's over,
That pushed him this far.

Then he hits the street
A sickening 'crack'!
His life has ended,
He's broken his back.

You think this is sad? This is not unique,
For bullies can make a lot of lives bleak . . .

Siân Watson (14)
Wreake Valley Community College

From Love To Hate

Love is gracious, love is kind,
Love requires a peace of mind.
Love is caring, love is true,
It's something that we all can do.

Love is honest, love is real,
'In love' is how we all can feel.
Love is tempting, love is fair,
Everything you own you share.

But . . .

Hate is evil, hate is bad,
Hate creeps up and makes you sad.
Hate is dreadful, hate is wrong,
It stays in your mind like an awful song.

Hate is horrid, hate is a fear,
Hate can also bring a tear.
Hate is nasty, hate means war,
What do we really *need* hate for?

Emma O'Mahony (12)
Wreake Valley Community College

Hallowe'en!

Rat-a-tat-tat
Who was that?
I opened the door
I saw a witch, maybe even more.

Her nose was big and crooked
Her teeth were yellow and chipped
Her hair was long and matted
Her skin was green and scaly
Her voice was very croaky
And she said to me -

'Scab matter custard
Cold phlegm pies
Dead dogs' giblets
Green cats' eyes

Snot on bread smeared on thick
All goes down with a cup of hot sick
Ha, ha, ha,' she cackled.

She disappeared in front of my eyes
All I could see was the moonlit sky
Was she real? Was she not?
I don't know what is what.

Hannah Kirton-Smith (12)
Wreake Valley Community College

The Bear Fright

I awoke with a terrible fright,
When on went my new blue light,
And there in the lovely clean air
Was a very fierce grizzly bear.

He drifted so slowly towards me,
I heard his laugh, 'Hee, hee, hee!'
I screamed so very loudly,
I really just couldn't sleep soundly.

He pounced on the quilt of my bed.
He crumpled it up, eager to be fed.
I fell on my laminate floor,
I just couldn't take this anymore.

He followed me down, his breath stank.
My sister at her friend's, my parents at the bank.
Home all alone and nobody to help.
He stood on my toe, I gave out a yelp.

I hopped round my room,
The storm in the garden, *boom!*
I woke up for real in bed,
Phew! The grizzly bear's dead!

Sabrina Smith (12)
Wreake Valley Community College

The Kids Of The Den

One afternoon after school,
The kids decided to play in the pool,
After the pool the kids were bored,
By the time the drinks were finally poured,
So they went outside to find a den.

Off they went by the factories,
Walking by a load of batteries,
Up to the forest looking for a den,
Which would be suitable for Ben,
He saw a den which made him addicted.

Ben shouted, 'That one,'
While it had the others in a con,
They entered with care,
To find food to spare,
And the food jumped up and bit their hair.

This freaked them out,
They all wanted to shout,
But the monsters defamed them,
With their long stringy phlegm,
And two of them choked to their death.

The three that did remain,
Were in a lot of pain,
But they managed to break through,
And one lost a shoe,
Then trod in a big pile of poo.

They followed Jack towards the black,
But the other two fell down the crack,
The monster was close, he could hear his fang,
But all of a sudden there was a *bang!*
He was gone and the kids of the den
        were never heard or spoken about again!

Liam Basi (12)
Wreake Valley Community College

Friendship

You're my friend and I'm here to say,
Our friendship grows stronger through each passing day,
You're here to comfort me through worry and strife,
You're here to help me along my path of life.

But if our friendship grows so far apart,
When there is little love for each other in our hearts,
I want you to know, I want you to hear me say,
I will be here for you each and every day.

I'd like you to know now before our time has passed,
That I had hoped beyond hope that our friendship will last,
I wish for this more than the world, you see,
Because you're my friend, my idol, my reason to be.

Laura Seaton (17)
Wreake Valley Community College

Are You Listening?

I sit and speak the truth to you,
Unaltered and unchanged.
The words I say come back to me,
Tampered with, deranged.

The pain I feel is deep within,
And there that pain must stay.
Locked up inside, where no one sees,
Hid from the light of day.

And yet the truth I still will speak,
My heart lies open, bare!
My love will show you nothing less,
That's how you know I care.

You think you are untouchable,
And yet that can't be true.
You've taken in the words I've said,
I know that I've touched you.

Amy Croxon (18)
Wreake Valley Community College

Aboard The Train To Hell

I found you early this morning,
In peace so deep.
Last night is a little blurry,
But you lie here fast asleep

You're sleeping on your stomach,
But I love to see your face,
When you're deep in slumber,
My heart begins to race.

I turn you on your back,
And I can't feel you breathing,
My hands are red with blood,
Why isn't your heart beating?

Then I see the wound!
It must have ended your life.
There's blood all over the bed,
And a trail that leads to the knife.

Cold beads of sweat trickle down my face,
As I recall the events of last night.
You told me you didn't love me anymore,
Which ended in a fight.

I stabbed you here . . . and here . . .
I was the Devil in disguise.
Your piercing screams are in my mind,
Your pleading and your cries.

Now I'm all alone, and I'm so filled with fear.
My eyes begin to water, as I hold you near.

I want to apologise to you up in Heaven,
Because I can still hear you yell.
But I can't see you right now
Because I'm aboard the train to Hell!

Kamal Bhana (15)
Wreake Valley Community College

The Night!

Ripples take over the surface of the lake
As a warty toad plops into the depths
The smooth skin pitch-black, reflecting the great moon
Orb-like stars scatter the sky, winking cheerfully.

Elegant leaves stretch out, aching for daylight
A minuscule fly with delicate wings
Swooping queasily through the air, dodging webs
Speckled with globes of rainwater, reflecting stars.

A crescent moon, stunning the Earth beneath it
A tiny planet made up of malice
The people of Earth do not deserve this gift
As the moon bathes the Earth in a golden twilight.

Eyes open and pupils widen as darkness
Overwhelms those who awake in the night
Their eyes white as eggs against the pitch-blackness
And when sleep beckons, their eyelids close yet again.

Soon a bird screech signifies the dawn chorus
The flowers spread their relieved petals wide
As the daylight drowns the silence of the night
The peace and calmness of the dark is no longer.

The day belongs rightfully to the humans
And the night is glad to own the great stars
The everlasting universe of silence
And the secrecy of the calm it hides with pride.

Hannah Clarke (12)
Wreake Valley Community College

My Night

The stars waved,
The moon smiled,
The sky stared,
And I stared too.

The owl screeched,
The mouse nibbled,
The rabbits slept,
And I slept too.

The trees swayed,
The leaves danced,
The flowers stirred,
And I stirred too.

The wind whispered,
The clouds blew,
The air coldened,
And I coldened too.

The air got warmer
The sun got higher
The morning woke up
And I woke up too

The stars disappeared,
The rabbits woke,
The owl flew home,
And I did too.

Gemma Bowey (13)
Wreake Valley Community College

The Coming Of The Moon

The sky is a beautiful tranquil turquoise,
Perfect in its high loneliness,
Crisp and fresh,

Like the first timid dawn that dared to peep out of the darkness,
So alive,
Yet so sad.

Waiting for the dark feathers of the night to sweep down upon it,
Twisting and turning in their eagerness to engulf it,
Writhing and coiling,

Like angry serpents reaching out to caress its faint fingers
                                    with their fangs,
As it bows down in acceptance of its fate,
Marooned in sadness.

Terrified in the knowledge of what is to come,
Even as the darkness weaves its jet-black shroud around it,
Smothering out existence.

Leaving only the smallest pinholes of light,
It turns a bright ghostly white
Not the colour of snow or of swans' feathers,
But of death,

        Of the moon!

Rebecca Frake (12)
Wreake Valley Community College

The Monster!

Beneath the covers, mattress and me,
There's something hiding in *my* territory,
It's been under my bed since I was a child,
It could be tame, or maybe wild.

I'm not sure what it looks like,
I only know it's there,
It haunts me dark 'til dawn,
Every child's nightmare.

It lives amongst the spiders and dust,
Oh how it gives me the creeps!
When I'm feeling extra brave,
I take a sneaky peep.

It could be green or maybe red,
Or possibly blue,
How many eyes, one hundred?
Or only one or two?

Perhaps it's as soft as silk,
Or even huge and hairy,
I know it's there beneath my quilt,
And I find it super scary.

One day when I am older,
Maybe nine or ten,
I'll look under my mattress,
And find out what's there then.

Hannah Johnston (12)
Wreake Valley Community College

Night-Time Blacksmith

Night is nasty, sleek and sly,
Makes all little children cry,
It lives in the attic under games and boxes,
It is a burglar like all foxes.

The eerie cry of witches,
Rats creeping in the ditches,
The darkness covers the Doomsday wood,
Run home, little children, as you should.

The rain came down hard and fast,
No one knew if it would last,
The blacksmith worked in his shed all night,
The night crept up on him with a fright.

He could not find his way back,
In the dark, a sheet of black,
Finding his way in the dark was hard,
The night was like a permanent guard.

But then when the morning's here,
Slowly lift away your fear,
Come out children, do not be afraid,
Night-time is where all your fears are made!

Grace Corby (12)
Wreake Valley Community College

Autumn

Autumn leaves come tumbling down,
Bright yellow colours hit the ground,
Orange, brown, even crimson,
Make a crinkly carpet to lie on.

Cock pheasants shine autumn colours,
Hiding in the shrubs and coverts,
Here comes Dad with the gun,
Bang, bang! Down one comes.

Berries are ripe, black and blue,
Best medicine if you've got the flu,
Mushrooms grow in the dew,
Must pick early, there's only a few.

Bonfires glow in the dark,
Fireworks explode with a giant spark,
Toffee apples, crunchy and so sweet,
At the end, autumn's hard to beat!

James Troop (12)
Wreake Valley Community College

The Motorbike

The fast, furious beast
Flying around the track
The sight is such a feast
There's no looking back.

The engine is so loud
Like the lion's roar
Moving like a cloud
As fast as a power saw.

The colours are such a sight
The blue, the green and the red
The fastest thing, it's such a fright
It will leave you standing dead.

The back end comes round
The front end comes up
His knee's touching the ground
The guy's after this cup.

As he crosses that finish line
And the motorbike is cooling down
This race was done in record time
The trophy is like a crown.

Bobby Large (12)
Wreake Valley Community College